The process is the price…4

Back to the Beginning…34

They Knew Not………42

The Residue Is a Sign…55

Late………………..70

Who is That………….77

Roles and Models……83

Time to Learn……….. 91

Heart Issues………..106

Keep It Moving……123

God Knows…..128

The Remedy…..135

The Power of Your Birth Right.153

A Higher Wisdom…..176

Chapter 1

The Process Is the Price.

I thought it was over! I sincerely believed that after I released my first book, I would never have to relive the pain that I experienced in my life. But truth be told, the advice to not take my medicine because I was healed and would never have to take it backfired. There I lay in another psychiatric unit after showing out all day. I was tired. I was broken again. I was just as baffled as the first time. How did I end up back here. I was back in the place that was prophesied and promised would never happen again. I was angry. I was bitter. I was hurt. But most of all I was scared. Was this going to end right? Or would I be committed to a state facility? I thought it was never going to be like it was. But there I sat in a cell-like environment with a steel toilet that still makes my face contort, to this day, at the thought of how disgusting it was in full disbelief. I had to go back to a hospital but this time I wasn't in Florida where all or most of my family lives. This time I was in Texas. I had never lived permanently away from my family for over an entire month and a half. This was my first time. As crazy as it sounds, I convinced my wife after hearing a million confirmations that God wanted us in Texas. We heard it on the television, we heard it on Tiktok.com, we heard it in many Facebook.com posts on our friends list. It was ringing all around us. We even got a word from a man of God from my hometown that God was getting ready to relocate us around likeminded people. We were scared but my wife being the best wife that I could ever ask for believed that this was the move that God had for us. She resigned from her school position, and we took everything we had and moved to the state of Texas. We found an extended stay kitchenette and we tried our best to live again after all that we had endured in Florida. I had not taken my medicine in over 3 months. And though I really believed that I was cured, all the symptoms of psychosis began to come back. I was dreaming more vividly. And my dreams became waking visions. It was just like the scene in a movie. I saw people, angels, and I saw a lion and a lamb in a deep night vision. I saw the King! I dreamed one night Jesus came through the roof of the hotel we were residing in and hugging me. All I can say is that may seem abnormal for a lot of people, but this was the reality that I experienced. It was very real to me. I can only tell it like it was. Believe me or not the visions were so clear, and I could see so well into the spirit realm. I was told that I had a prophetic gift of a Seer. This was more than I could handle. In the natural I experienced and entirely different reality. My visions landed me in a psychiatric facility for 5 days away from family and away from my wife. It felt like I was in jail. It was cold. There were strange people all around.

My wife tells me that I was loud belligerent and forcefully cursing people who had hurt me the most out. I was jumping up and down. I was threatening, I was irrational. I was hearing and seeing hallucinations. I was out of my right mind! As sad as it sounds it would only take those who know me personally and academically and even from church to know that this was abnormal activity for me. This was not my first rodeo. I have been here so many times. The police were called, I was arrested by 6 men and put into an ambulance. I was not a criminal but, in these situations, you get treated like one for fear of self-harm possibly becoming a threat to others. I was terrified! To me this was the reality that I would never relive because of all the prophesies and words ministered to me. People know in part as the bible says. This means they (spiritual people) don't know everything; many did not go through this nightmare I went through over and over for 15 years in and out of psych facilities. If I sound bitter, please forgive me. But this is my only chance to release the absolute rage I felt inside for my problems,

I had so many questions. I never understood how the righteous could feel so forsaken. I never understood the many afflictions that the Lord promised to deliver me out of, so I pouted and cried. Not only because of my circumstances but because God allowed them. He could have stopped it all in an instant but He allowed me to go through so I could tell someone on the other side there is hope. You are not alone. God is still good. You can make it if you just believe! This happened because of a misunderstanding that I had about the leaders in the church. I went through what I thought to be spiritual abuse because of a misunderstanding thinking that leadership was God. They may have the word of God and they may be used by God, but God alone is God. We are to obey the leaders do not worship them. Do not hold them to a standard that humans should never be. I had to learn to forgive the very people that hurt me in the church. They did not mean to, and I understand now that no parent has a manual. They are learning to be a parent even as you are learning to be a child. When we got to Dallas, Texas my wife and I were led to sow seeds of money for financial breakthrough. I believed God would and he still can. But why would I have to give money to a minister to get them. That's the immaturity and the ignorance that I thought in my carnal mind. I was not fully understanding the principal, or the process of God.

He had to strip us to allow us to fully understand He was going to turn the situation around. He never needs our help to bless us. He needs our cooperation and obedience. Obedience is better than sacrifice! I was in a cloudy head space because I had been taking my medications consistently for years and as a result, I was sound in my mind and believed that psychosis would have never happen again. After trusting God and trying to understand why He would lead us to a new state and to sow financial seeds, we got down to a negative account balance in less than 2 weeks from thousands to zero. Sounds like a God thing to me. You see with thousands God can't do it! He needs zero dollars in your account! None of you! All of Him! Gideon the man in the bible went to battle thinking that God needed all the soldiers he had until God made him cut the army down from 32,000 soldiers to 300 warriors! They won not by might nor by power but by the spirit of the Lord! That is the scene that this psychotic breakdown surrounded. I was hurt on the inside. I was mad. I was literally experiencing the horror of being angry with the process of God and I felt in my mind I was being taken advantage of. If was not in a manic state off my medicine, which often leads to my psychotic breaks, none of this would have happened or so I thought. But it did! I was not being used! The enemy was using me! Manipulation at its finest. Now I sat in this jail-like facility rocking back and forward. Scared that this place was hell. Thinking that I just had died. I thought my mental stuff was dealt with, I thought it was over, but I was just getting to the core of my problem. My process was long but with every dark cloud comes a silver lining. It wasn't over. In many ways it was just the beginning. It was a time for me to reflect on the experiences that brought me to such a bleak and dark existence. I still had to deal with me! The grace of God and mercy was this that even though I was in the hospital I found myself, preaching in the hospital and sharing my testimony with others. It wasn't over yet; the process was going to another level and so was the anointing in my life!

After sharing my testimony and writing my first book, digging up old feelings and this time, having to deal with them seemed harder than writing the first time. I had to look at my trauma for what it was, I had to understand the outcomes of exposing my experiences of sexual, physical, emotional, psychological abuse, and neglect. I had to face the music. It was the most difficult time. More hurtful than the events themselves. It was at this point that I realized that I had to come out of my pit. I had to tell it all. Releasing my first book was difficult. It was the crack in the door that led the flood gates wide open. This is why I was so reluctant to share. As I continue to do the work of healing. I discovered that the pain had layers and dimensions that I never knew. The real revelation was that healing comes in waves. Being healed from traumatic life situations involves levels of openness which bring forth freedom. Openness comes in stages, and it comes with trusting that the people you are opening yourself up to heal.

The revelation that I needed more healing all started when I was listening to a story of a victim of sex re assignment surgery. There was a clip of a young lady (born male) that surfaced on YouTube. This story was so moving, because the person was victimized by being encouraged to undergo medical surgery to reassign him as a female. The person, just like me, dealt with severe gender dysphoria. This gender dysphoria happens when you feel different from the sex male or female that you were assigned at birth. This spirit of delusion happens to people mostly from childhood. It happens so early on the person does not know where it starts and believes that it was their identity from birth. This is why it is said, I was born this way. I didn't realize that this was the cause of my childhood depression. I felt mixed matched inside of my body. Also, after being sexually abused by males made me later feel like a series of questions that brewed in my mind. Did they pick up that I had these feelings of wanting to be female? Did that provoke them to do sexually abusive things to me because they thought that they could take a chance to make me their secret? Most importantly, was all this my fault? I was so confused, but I began to get clarity from this interview. so compelling that I immediately did an inventory in my own mind about how people could be so inhumane by taking advantage of someone that was so broken. The person on YouTube ended up sick and maimed from this surgery that had to be performed 2-3 times to correct the previous operation. I cried for this individual. I knew this person never wanted this. This person only wanted relief in their mind.

Relief from the torment that comes with a condition of a stolen identity. This happens to most transgender people.

During that night, which was hours after I had heard the story, I woke up out of my sleep and immediately went to my phone to research what was on my mind as I often do. What I found while looking on a sexual abuse victim site was disturbing to say the least. Although, I knew that I had endured abuse because of trauma and being exposed to adult things at a young age, even suffering with a severe mental illness because of those things, but what I did not know was what I discovered that night. I wasn't only a victim. I was targeted. I uncovered deep layers of unresolved issues. I had all these feelings of shame, guilt, depression, emptiness, numbness, and most importantly what I would later was the most hidden. I discovered the hidden RAGE!?!? I smiled all the time. No one on the outside knew. It was all a big secret that led to the fire in my chest. I was victimized sexually by people I knew. This made me sicker in my stomach than the thought of what happened to me. I began to remember all the things that I had tried to forget. This was my first step in getting free again.

My first published book was a light touch of what took place but this time I got to tell everything. Healing is not an event. It is a lifestyle. It is a choice to live. It is a decision to feel the pain. Process it and let it go. It is a chance to refuse to quit and die because of the pain you endured. Unearthing the seemingly hidden reality was tough. Although I sincerely desire to cover the people involved because this book is not a bash book. I don't want anyone or force anyone to feel bad or sorry for me. I found out that most of the people who traumatized me were victims and they did to me what others did to them. As sad as it is I hurt inside for their situations. I can only imagine the sheer torture that they experience knowing what they did to me and others. I know mine. I'm here to reclaim my peace, and as I discovered in my last book, telling my story is my way out so I need to tell it with confidence that it will reach the right person who needs to hear and heal. I want to impact as many people as I can and let them know they are not alone. They don't have to want to die in their heads every night! There is so much to live for! My experience of gender dysphoria leading to thoughts of transgenderism, it is trying to find a resolution by sort of killing the part of you that was abused and tormented to rebirth yourself into confidence. That is the appeal of it! This is my story, I want to give those who struggle with gender identity, especially the ones who suffered sexual abuse tools to survive and even thrive after such a horrible lie from the enemy that creates these situations. The story I now unveil in one that is so necessary because it is my freedom song. I can now dance in the truth. I possess the power to breathe with the kind of freedom that I must no longer hate myself or feel the intense shame and filthiness within my soul. There are many LGBTQIA identified individuals who have never been sexually assaulted to their knowledge. I am in no way insinuating that his happened because of my abusive history but I am saying the scars from those abuses initially tormented me to the point of death by self-harm. I now stand unashamed, knowing this is my story and it will get better. This is my way to fight through it all and scream to the world… I will live

and not die!

Chapter 2

Back to the Beginning

I was a small kid who was always called the teacher's favorite. I worked hard to make people happy. I even assumed the role of a comedian so to speak to my family… My family… My family was where things were often toughest for me. These are the people who I loved the most that caused the most pain. For years I never told a soul and I know everyone says that what happens at home is supposed to stay at home, but what happens when what happened at home spews out of control causing the onset of mental illness? Do I allow what they did to consume me? Do I allow it to stay shut up in me and cause me to die in silence as a result? I got to fight. This is for the people who may never feel their courage to tell their story. I am here to drag the bones out of our closets, especially the bones that were broken by the words and actions that were not supposed to hurt us.

Although I never knew I was a fighter I had to learn how to fight. I had to fight myself and everything and everyone around me to find my voice and tell the truth. For once I had to cry because I was hurt. Yes, they hurt me! They mistreated me. I'm even the victim of child-on-child sexual abuse by multiple people. The hardest thing to stomach in this was that I had to realize was a victim of incest which means family sexual abuse. This revelation once realized, almost killed me! I felt more disgusted. I did not want to live with the ugly scent of that phrase. The residue of the memory of what took place with people I made excuses for almost threatened to break me beyond repair. It was enough that I was harassed and called a faggot for being different and a gentle soul, I had to go through being seduced as a child into lewd acts. I had forgotten the times that I was touched inappropriately at daycare, at school, and at home and at relatives' homes. As the memories surfaced, they kept playing over and over in my head. I was called faggot so many times I can't count.

That memory was still locked in the fibers of my being. I couldn't breathe.

I was physically victimized also and was made to be fearful. I did not know how to fight back. I felt powerless. I was afraid. I couldn't talk. I was pushed and shoved. I was psychologically abused and told that I was weak for being a scared little boy. I was the victim. However, I masked the pain through a smile and laughter. I walked away many times not even knowing that I was taken advantage of, I had every right to get even, I didn't I just kept quiet and pretended like everything was ok.

For years I thought it was all my fault. This doesn't happen to everyone, right? This is my past and my experience because I was the reason I became a target, right? I made myself a target because I was different, right? All the questions were beginning to pour out of myself and because I did nothing to stop these events I felt like the victim and perpetrator. It hurt me more than anyone could

ever imagine.

Chapter 3

They Knew Not

Did you know that the people that hurt you even in the slightest of ways may not truly know or remember what they did to you or how it impacted you. They don't know the sleepless nights they caused you. Or that the residue of what took place made you the shell of your former self. I want to let you in on a little secret, It's not about them! This one is on you. It is the lesson on forgiveness that is vital for your growth, mental health, and physiological wellbeing. Forgiveness is the gift you give yourself to move on and get past the hurt. Forgiveness is a mindset that only winners understand. You can't drive a car fixated on the rear-view mirror. We must look forward to moving forward from the past. Declare today that enough is enough, my freedom is no longer attached to an apology that I may never hear from those who played a part in my pain. Before they apologize or make amends, set your heart to forgive. According to the bible we cannot expect to be forgiven by the

Father in heaven if we don't' forgive people who hurts us. Those who perpetrated the crime against you may never pay for what they did in your presence, but you pay by holding on to it. If you don't swiftly forgive you, you become self-destructive and a self-sabotaging person. Often recreating the feelings of hurt which is self-abuse to keep the memory of what they did alive only hinders you. The person who did you wrong is free living their lives they forgot the stain they

16

gave you. The heart break they caused you is only remembered by you. There you are bound stuck and confused about something you didn't even cause. The only way to be free from torment, you must let it go, so that it can let you go. No need to wake up every night and be reminded of what was taken from you. You have the power to tell your mind how to think. You have authority over your mind. When you speak out loud your mind will automatically get quiet because the spoken word has the power to stop the enemy in you from torturing you, which comes from reliving the experience. The replay reopens the wounds every time you keep the memory fresh. It is bound to hurt you again!

Yes, it happened, and it did not feel good. Yes, the person who did it should make up for it, but my question to you why keep suffering? Do you believe that you have been given the authority to stop the pain by letting go of the situation. I wonder could holding on to your past hurts make sense to you because you have become so used to the pain that you have fallen in love with your abuser. Meaning the more you hold on to the abusive things that took place, when it becomes time to move on and get free you are afraid of fully laying down this grudge because you have become more open to the idea of keeping it inside.

Somewhere in my mind and in the mind of many people who were molested as children, there is a thought that it was their fault and somewhere that may make you feel that you deserved the abuse. Truth be told, you don't need their apology to give you permission to have peace.

Forgiveness is a real gift toward growth when you give yourself the gift or inner release before you ever hear I am sorry for what I did from the perpetrator. Stop the cycle! Get off the Farris wheel of regret, take the helm of the ship and stir clear of the iceberg in the water. It may seem small on the surface but the titanic proved to us all that what peeps up at the surface rarely reveals the mass of danger that lies beneath. You will fly once you release the baggage and realize that hurt people repeat cycles that they didn't create. Don't become your offender! Let go of the offense. That is how I healed. One step at a time. Releasing one memory at a time. Stepping into the new me one day at a time.

Jesus, while being crucified said Father forgive them for, they know not what they do. In the bible, in the book of Ephesians it teaches believers that we are not supposed to wrestle or fight with people, because there are spiritual forces that uses people without them knowing they are being used by a force to create chaos in the lives of others. It is my job if I want to be free to release myself from being stuck by saying its ok you don't have to pay for what they did and telling myself I refuse to pay for what I did. No one can stop a person who can forgive! Forgiveness is a superpower. It is letting go of the past that will help you get to your destination. You must erase his name. The name of the abuser, and you must allow God to rewrite your story. Take that offender out of the prison that you feel they deserve. I tell you the truth if you don't you will sit in the cell with the perpetrator every day trying to rationalize holding unforgiveness.

We have a finite mind. There are only so many memories that we will have in this brain, do not waste another millimeter in your brain to conjure dark feelings of how the one who did you wrong should pay for their crime against you. Your mind was never supposed to be a dungeon, but it becomes a jail cell when you lock in it all the people that hurt you. Let it Go! It is your time to stop crying over the occurrence. Find joy by starting to laugh at the strength value and vitality that comes on the other side of pain. That is when you endure pain it will fuel your purpose. This is the place that joy lives and this is how I found out Jesus was a true example from birth to death even to the resurrection of the dead. That dead weight must go. This is how the phoenix in you can arise from the ashes! It is time to show how resilient you are through the love of Jesus! He will allow you to recreate the unstoppable you.

Chapter 4

The Residue Is a Sign

The signs that you have not totally forgiven could be the thought at 3:00 am I can't sleep… because I am awake!

For years you can think that you are mentally strong and that you can handle anything. You can assume that because there is no bruise or no bleeding that what happened did not hurt you. Today, I need you to wake up, you have endured severe trauma! You may not even know this is the case.

Physical abuse can be very upsetting, but the worst abuse to me is mental abuse. When people play on your mind it is easy to turn on yourself and begin to tell yourself lies. You may think seeing a sleeping dog in a bed is peaceful. Just because his eyes and his mouth are closed you assume you're not in danger. This is very deceptive, because although you haven't surfaced that deep rooted hurt yet, it is still there! It is just dormant. It is sleep. Not only does unresolved trauma have the power to hurt you it can cause unnecessary and premature death. It is why that heartbeat of yours has become irregular, and the reason that cancer might get the chance to creep up on you. It is just that serious! For me, it put me in a prison of my mind, I was locked up so badly in my mind that every mental hospital I stayed in look like a jail to me. It was jail. The police put handcuffs on me although I committed no crime. I understand they had to constrain me to keep me from hurting myself or them. But the mental abuse showed me that words have the power to create a world. I thought it was my fault because of the disease in my mind. Now I know that I can gain power over every part of the pain. Even the residue! The small night terrors are under my authority through the power of the cleansing blood of Jesus! He gave me the authority in His name to claim victory, this is how you possess the power to win over those negative thoughts.

They hurt you! Consequently, you can reoffend yourself if you let it fester. Now you hold the smoking gun! You have become no better than they are. It takes careful observation to realize that unresolved trauma is sending you messages all the time. It is in how uptight you are. It lives in the racing thoughts at night. It is in the anxiety that you feel when you can't control everything. It is in the quitting when things become overwhelming. For years I, constantly quit jobs because I was overwhelmed. Once I realized I had never completed anything because all my mental energy went towards holding my perpetrators in my memories. I was tired. Too tired to do what I wanted to do because we only have so much energy and the weight of my past was holding me back from accomplishing any attainable goal. The residue is often small and subtle. Here is a small indication you have unresolved issues, when you won't ever take a compliment without saying "yeah but," to everything! This is often followed by turning the compliment into more negativity because you don't want to accept it. It was just a compliment! Stop it now! Admit it! It is not everyone's fault that someone else hurt you deeply! You were a victim of a heinous crime. It was molestation, it was rape, it was physical abuse, it was word that broke you. But you can be fixed, healed, and delivered and restored to life in Jesus Name! Jesus is the healer, but you have to allow him into the pain! He wants to share the burden and give you, his peace!

Dealing with the residue, I had to accept the fact that nonconsensual sex is abuse. I was underage and I didn't know what it was. My innocence was stolen. The violation continues unknowingly because of innocence and ignorance. When a perpetrator is skilled in the art of manipulation, they can be so sneaky that the abuse doesn't hurt the body, but years later it is painful to the soul. It left invisible scars and mental chains that keep you bound years after it happened. It might have even felt so good, too good for a young child to see it as a bad touch. That's how shame buries itself in your soul. You thought it was your fault. Shame on you! You should have known better. This is what tries to convince you that even as a child until this day you told yourself in your mind, I should have stopped it! I should have told someone! The truth is you didn't know that you were being taken advantage of. You didn't know that you were being groomed. It didn't hurt then, but it does now!

Reading this you may still be in denial, but your uncomfortableness is betraying you. Your energy is telling a story, and that is what has kept healing far from you. I didn't realize the effects of my abuse until I got married the second time. I was in my 30's when I realized that when my wife would try to touch me lovingly, I felt pain! The kind of pain that felt severely uncomfortable. I would snatch away. I would feel forced to act like I liked it so I wouldn't reject her. Inside I wanted and needed her touch but in the confusion of my mind, I didn't like how it made me feel. Especially when she didn't alert me before she touched me. It was a sign! I was blind to the fact that the reason I didn't like her healthy touch was because of the many unsolicited and inappropriate touches I had received. I was a rape victim. I was nasty, and dirty, and ugly, and unlovable! People don't know how sexual abuse of children really sets the person up for a life of dysfunction.

For years, I was sleeping on the fact of what happened, well until I woke up! It wasn't until then that I could address the severe abuses I received. Often it isn't a strange danger. It is the people that were in proximity. Letting guards down with people thinking that they would never hurt me was very wrong. A harsh lesson to learn as a minor! These were the very people that taught me not to trust. Their words cursed me. Their actions scared me. Their secrets imprisoned me. There I was in darkness. I couldn't sleep. 3:00 am 4:00am, 5:00 am. It wasn't my sleep that was broken, it was my peace!

The very thoughts of what took place decades ago held the sleeper in me and made me a hostage victim, forcing me to stay awake. It was the fact that I believed the names they called me. It was the fact that I wore the shame they clothed me with. I gained weight! Now over 400lbs and looking like a bear. But feeling like a wimp, I could no longer hibernate like a bear because the little boy in my soul was awakened to the fact that I was a victim, I couldn't sleep because it was time to do my work of healing. I had to find the way to become totally victorious.

Chapter 5

Late

Midnight is where I got most revelation about childhood trauma. I had to do something about all the revelations I received. Even coming to terms with how sick my mind became. I could not admit to myself that they really did a number on me. I had to find a way to untie the knots that were in my stomach when I thought about the fact that not only was I a victim of sexual abuse it was several abuses on top of each other. Shame entered my mind at this very moment. I would have to shut my mouth and keep it a secret. Certain communities of people are built on codes of secrecy and that is why they will stay bound and broken. Nothing changed until I chose freedom, better yet freedom chose me.

When my apology came from some of the people responsible it didn't help at all, it only quieted the questions temporarily, and silenced the trauma response long enough for me to catch some more zzzz's and sleep another decade of my life away in and out of mental hospitals seeking treatment for the hurt that "they" caused. Sorry isn't good enough. Try replacing the income from the years that I couldn't keep a job. Try buying a house… That could help, least you could do after you had stolen my sense of home. Either way, I had to move on and keep pushing. Without retribution from those who caused so much pain I had to move on. They had the power to mess my life up, but only God could provide the tools to fix it.

Struggling to sleep. I have tossed and turned, including taking two melatonin gummies at times, but I was still up! It's ok now, I had to find my way to work out my deliverance. Writing my way to freedom. Writing is a great tool. I have healed way more in writing than doing any other task so in my waking moments I know it's time to write. It was in writing that I got my release. My soul knew that it needed to find a voice. When I couldn't sleep because it would not allow me to sleep, I learned writing was the gift that the pain brought forward. I needed to say what I needed to say. It was late by I finally got myself to sleep. Only words could soothe my soul. By saying some things in this book that I couldn't say to anyone in a therapy session, or in church. Right now, I can say for sure, the rage is gone! It left a few paragraphs ago. The residue is dissipating. With each word I write my eyelids get heavier. I awake the next morning. I made it through my midnight, and you can too. It is

a brand-new day!

Chapter 6

Who Is That?

Sometimes we erroneously learn wrong lessons. I was taught that I am nobody. This lie causes so much damage because if I am nobody I don't matter. I am not a threat. I don't count. This changed one day I found out my voice does matter. I was 13 when I sat at my grandmother's dinner table, and she asked me what I wanted to eat that night. I said oh it doesn't matter. It was then that she as the councilor because she had been a school counselor, had risen to teach me a lesson through her experiences, she said it does matter! What you like does matter! That very second, she gave me a lesson in finding me. I was the youngest of 5. I was seemingly laid back and went with the flow so long trying not to upset the apricot, that I had lost myself in the identity of others. It didn't matter to me because what mattered to me was keeping peace and not causing trouble. There was enough rage and violence going on at home I didn't want to add a pin drop to the chaos. In my attempt to create an environment of ease I had chosen early on to not be a fighter. I felt if I ever started fighting, I would never be able to stop! When things happened to me or were said about me or done to me, I erroneously just took it as, ok. However, my journey has taught me, it is not ok! I needed people to stand up for me to demonstrate I was important enough for a change. I mattered! A seed was planted in me during moments of hardship. This was a seed of love. It made me want to grow up and be a dad one day. I wanted people to feel safe around me. For the years that I felt unsafe around others. Safety! That is one great thing about men who are protectors we do so because protection is vital. Protection reminds us that we are valuable.

There were a lot of disagreements in my household. The constant arguments my family endured made me feel everything but safe, I always wished it would stop. In school I was chosen as a safety kid. I loved school, there in the thick concrete walls I could truly say I felt a sense of safety. I found that as a man you are naturally a protector. It is your job to provide others with a sense of safety. At school I felt safe, sometimes I had to make a choice to die or fight to live even in school. It was my heritage to excel in school and was a straight A student during many school terms because education was strongly promoted by my dad.

Chapter 7

Roles and Models

A boy's dad is very important in his life. As a male we need role models for identity. My dad taught me well about the ills of life. He explained to me and my brothers how tough this world was. He saved me a lot of headaches by preaching the truth to us consistently. He said the more you know the further you go. He also would say knowledge is power. Read your bible and do your push-ups. I am just now realizing that this advice was for me as a man to be strong both spiritually and physically that I could protect my family. That I could provide them a word from God of clarity and peace as well as cause peace to happen physically. In writing, I really understood that my father was the catalyst for my becoming a minister! Many times, when events occur, they happen because everyone involved was a victim of the circumstances. The older I get I realize that the people that tampered with my innocence and created craters in my soul were people that the very same thing happened to. I, just like my dad had, found compassion for those who caused me harm. I had let go of the pain and I had become a protector of the innocence of others. I was healing. I was being used strategically in healing others. My life became a source of help. I became free. Anger ends where love begins. According to the Bible love covers a multitude of sins. This is my freedom and my testimony. I can share with the world, and that is precisely what I plan to do.

Putting my mind in the position to see what the people who hurt me had gone through helped me. It granted me another gift called compassion. Thinking compassionately and in the shoes of those who hurt me gave me enough common sense not to point fingers. We all have made mistakes. Yes, it happened! Yes, it hurt! Yes, I lost my right mind!

But being mad and unforgiving to my family members and others was not the solution. It was the problem. I always felt hated by certain people. When I stopped and thought about why certain people seemingly hated me, and empathized with how they felt, I realized that I was in the way of the love they wanted so badly from each other. Trying to be perfect all the time was a problem because I was the baby who got all the attention in some people's minds. I became aware that other people have hurt that led them to the shameful and desperate decisions they made. In some of my relatives words they felt they had to fight me to fight for their seat at the table. They too felt neglected because of my existence. This was because of the appearance of the love I got from my mother. I found out this made them feel abandoned and neglected. To them I stole their mother's heart. I was a thief and I needed to pay a price and feel the hurt and pain how they did. Pain is a two-way street. I was not aware that I too caused people pain. This contributes to the constant back and forth between families.

When you are longing for something like love and affection, you will do anything to get it. The seed of rage and rape many times comes from the perpetrator's feelings that something was taken from them in their early lives. It is the hate they have exposed by violently acting out. I did not know that many perversions of life often are birthed from a lack of love and attention in childhood.

Chapter 8

Time To Learn… Time To Live

We must be more watchful of children. The command to go outside, and play can be a recipe for a disaster. This causes many memories that can take years to forget. It can happen early on with children that may not show signs of sexual activity. Typically, sexual desire which starts around puberty but for some time early on. Puberty only adds hormones to an already lit fire. Like gasoline being ignited a lot of damage can take place. We need to be informed of stages of development and abnormal patterns of growth.

For me a form of healing also took place when I had the courage to apologize to one of the people who molested me. I apologized because I realized they too felt victimized. They didn't know that this would happen. I wanted to free them! I know that in their right mind they would have never let it happen. Life is not a cookie cutter. Wrong is a two-way street. Consider your offender they too carry scars. This forgiveness could bring healing without a trace and bring you into the new.

~Life is not fair!~

I had to mature early on. I learned many life lessons that matured me prematurely. The self-discipline I often displayed was because of the maturity that came because I lacked the ability to receive the love of my father. I couldn't feel it because it was so different than a mother's love. We confuse the father's love with a soft and affectionate type of mushy love from mom. Instead of that type of gushy love, I felt the correction. This, I misinterpreted turning his truth that he was teaching us as hate, but now that I am becoming a man, I now know it was love. It was a father's love that loved me enough not to send me into the world ignorant and unarmed. It came hard and tough, but it was necessary. The world is often a war zone. You have got to be tough mentally. Or you will be eaten alive. I had to wise up! I had to be my own dad once my dad died. My father's role was to build me to become a better version of him so that when he died I would have enough of him in me to survive. The hours of lectures, the drilling, the forced push-ups, the cold stares, even being cussed out, all built me to be tough enough to make it through any storm. In the book of Proverbs in the bible, the writer says, "my son pay attention to my instructions." A good father tells a son how to dodge the bullets that got him hurt during his life. My daddy did that and it paid off in my life even until this day. Life isn't fair was the best lesson that he taught me. Suck it up and keep moving forward!

Weakness in you doesn't equate to throwing every part of you away! My wise father taught his sons about this world. With a smile on his face, my dad would often say I want to go home to see God and when I die make sure Charlie (Our cousin and Family

Funeral Director at the time) press a smile on my face, he would say! He was a soldier! He didn't mind being brave. He could care less about being a casualty if he knew he left his mark! He did just that! He left his mark with me and within me! I received the most from my father in my opinion. It was my esteemed pleasure to be there with my dad in his final days. He shared intimate details with me because he was saying I can trust you. He saw the minister in me, and I felt the honor of being a son.

I was the one he talked to about his failures. He even told me I was going to eulogize his funeral. He knew I could handle it. I was 20! He knew I could preach! He knew I could!

I never knew that when my dad heard me preach for the first time it gave him so much joy and pride that he bragged on me. He told everybody my son is a man of the cloth. One day when I was working with him, he told the other guys to respect me and not swear because I was a man of the cloth. I was 16. But he called me a man. I'm 36 now I just realized my dad called me a man at 16.

Another life altering experience was the death of my oldest brother. Before my oldest brother died which was very devastating to me, he told me that our father foretold my future to him when I was a toddler. My brother told me that my dad said I was his preacher before I became the person I am today. I was too young to remember, but my daddy prophesied my destiny. My daddy spiritually ordained me to deliver truth. To deliver him. To set him free. To set people free with the help of the Holy Spirit. I believe that my story in this book is allowing that to happen right now.

My first major ministry assignment was at my father's funeral. He didn't live to see me become who I am today, But I know he was proud at his funeral. I saw it on my brother's, cousin's, and uncle's faces. I saw that proud look of a father on all those strong black men that he imparted into.

That look was saying look at my son! Boy you bad! Preach that word all by yourself! Everyone there told me, boy you preached your daddy funeral! These words were exactly everyone's sentiment who encouraged me thereafter! They thought it was me, but I knew it was the Holy Spirit in me! The opportunity was my father's final gift to me! I now know, he gave me the power to be my own man! He may have failed in life, but this was the set up that I may win. He died, that I may live. He was disrespected by people that I may be honored! That was more than I could ever ask for!

To my father, who I learned more from than any other teacher, Daddy, I love you! I miss you and I know you smiling down! Your baby boy understands now! I get the sharp lessons that were sharp enough to cut my folly off just as the the foreskins of the children of the promise were commanded to be cut away! I am to am spiritually being circumcised now! My spiritual rite of passage is happening as I write this book. I see how your dedication to me, and the family earned you respect in the community. My dad has a building in my hometown dedicated to him! He deserved it and so much more! He was my hometown hero. I just wished He could be here to see his seeds attain unto the fullness of greatness that he prophesied. It is your time to make sure that you don't become your offender, let go of the offense. Honor every voice that is bringing you up and out of the pit of despair. That is how I healed. One step at a time. Releasing one memory at a time. Stepping into the new me one day at a time.

Chapter 9

Heart Issues

Have you ever had what you didn't want, yet wanted what you didn't have? It's like a paradox. Some of the most painful times in life is when you are mature enough to admit that the things that you fought for most in life are the things that will fight against coming to you. We must wait on the Lord to receive what He has for us! It is the madness of the way that life works that can drive us crazy trying to find what we already have.

Having lack is the place in which lust is nurtured. It is that place where the desire for something is so strong it overwhelms you, evoking passionate fantasies of having things which result in unfulfillment when you land back into reality of the lust not being enough. It leads to a life of discontent. You can never fulfil lust, it keeps demanding more and more, until you find yourself in places you never thought you would be. The strong lust may have been born from places of abuse. This created craters in your soul that you desire fulfillment in that will never be filled completely.

Having a divided heart was my issue. I wanted to live a happy life with all the things that I thought would make me happy. The question was what it would be like to never have had to struggle, this caused me severe torment. What would life be if I was a different person and never had to know this kind pain.

I was divided and I believed that the life I had was not the life I wanted. But wanting something is not all bad in my mind it was just discontentment. The truth is emptiness often propels us to action. Actions that are detrimental to the life we wish we have. It leads us to making bad decisions. These decisions can't be washed off with soap and water. They can jeopardize and compromise everything good in your life. You become a self-saboteur. It is the way inordinate way that we learn to pursue things. It is not good. I have encountered many setbacks because of self-sabotage. This is because of the heart that is divided and the effects of the divide. It creates hate in you for the blessings you do have. Just like that saying you can't see the forest for the trees, you can't see the good for the bad.

I had to learn how to deal with the fact that I always wished for a life other than my own. Maturing past the hurt feelings is what helped me. For one, I had to learn that having life is far greater than being dead. Being grateful and finding reasons to smile although I wanted things to be different there was a great benefit in finding contentment in the struggle. This was a better way of waiting on the Lord to add the stuff I wanted.

The main problem with lust is that it is never completely satisfied. For many the opening of the door to begin to try to please the desires of our heart that came from abuse ends up in addiction and bondage. It starts with a little and ends up in a state of greed, grief, and self-torment because of overindulgence. Then despite the many efforts to self-medicate we find the major problem, which is the heart is still not satisfied. You have eaten enough that you should be full, but the food is not filling because the hole is in your heart and not in your stomach. You still crave food even in the face of being stuffed. This is how you gain and gain weight because of unhealed and undealt with trauma.

You look at your life and you feel guilty that the feeling of satiety never comes when you are hurting. Now what? What can you do now that you went way past what you thought you would? It was the promise that you said, "I will eat only one slice," then you eat another and another next thing you know the pie is gone and you are looking for something else to fill you. Eating to find fulfillment becomes dangerous when eating for pleasure takes you out of feeling numb. You eat that way because it is the only way you can feel you. It becomes most detrimental when you realize that the real you is left untouched because the inner you is hiding under layers because you filled you to feel you.

I thought that my double minded ways came because of the lack of consistency in thought but I found out it was my divided heart that played the most important role in my instability. The instability of the heart is different than a double mind.

A double mind deals with the thoughts that turn and changes one's opinion often. The divided heart has two sets of feelings and emotions attached that create a dysfunctional life of going back and forward.

There is no way to rule out a double heart. A double mind can't consider logically the best route and plan of action, which is the place where one option beats the other option, and the divided heart simply cannot be conquered with logic. It must be trained and renewed by God's word in the bible. We must forget those negative experiences totally and that is how to fully get rid of the torture. The divided heart is deeply seated in the soul in the place where you feel that you are torn. But the Lord can put that divided heart back together and give you one mind. I am a living witness. It can be done. If He did it before for me, He can do it again and again! However, many times I remember, He can help me forget If I keep

Jesus as my focus, I will not drown in the abyss of my own past.

Oddly enough, there was a song that was very popular in the early 2000's. By the R&B group 702. The song says, "I don't really want to go I don't really want to stay, what I really need to know is can we get it together." The divided heart can't get it together! After all its apart and the main issue is not just that you have a divided heart, you have a divided love. You must be healed to move on. The feeling that you love it and you hate it at the same time is a tale-tale sign of the divisions in your heart. Refuse to live a life of self-betrayal because you fail to make up your heart (mind) to commit to one thing and hate the other. If you don't you may consequently become a slave to many masters, and that is the place you can lose your sense of identity.

Reclaiming your identity or knowing inherently who you are is a vital cure to a double or divided heart. When a person discovers who he or she is beyond the noise of everyone's opinions and advice, that is the epitome of making a true decision and following your heart. The heart of God can only be developed after being born again. This is when the heart filled with anger and abusive experiences truly gets healed. When you ask Jesus to become the king to sit on the throne of your heart. He will take the broken pieces and put it all together again to become the glory of God. This heart can never deceive you if you have patiently taken enough time to develop an ear to hear what the heart of God is truly saying. The message that this heart is conveying is what is the right way to go.

What keeps you alive and what is going to sustain life in the life that you live is Christ. Without Him this is the reason why the person who does not know Him or themselves gets into trouble and tortures themselves for years trying to find a way to be who they really are. Your authentic identity is in Christ. He knows what He created and the reason you were

created.

Chapter 10

Keep It Moving

In my life, my mind too was divided. I lived for others. I lived for the applause and the acceptance of family and the people who didn't have the ability to set their own souls free to be who they were to be in Christ. They were broken and wouldn't know love if it hit them square dead between the eyes and introduced itself. The truth of the matter is that they hated themselves because that is the human condition. We have a tendency toward self-hatred fueled by the lack of knowledge of how to forgive ourselves and others. The hate that they spewed on me out of ignorance was much more than they would have had time to understand. This fostered in me a pseudo reality and a self-hatred that threatened me to live a lie. I was a person who early on felt I knew who I was. This is not the full story. We can never be our full selves without being in the right relationship and fellowship with our creator. This means, I just had a sense of self, and I thought I knew where I was going before many people knew that life was ultimately going to take me to the wrong destination. I thought I knew who I wanted to be and what I wanted to do. The only thing is I wanted people to love me and go with me on the journey. This was the ultimate kryptonite; it was the Achilles heel that kept me from progressing. You can heal within, or you can make it seem impossible to get over what happened in your life. Is it impossible? Or is the price so high that you are not willing to pay it to

save your own life?

Chapter 11

God Knows

I had to realize that above all descriptions of God the most important is that God is love and God is life. God is the reason to live. He is life! So, while making excuses you must understand that being alive is the reason to live. Be you. Your authentic self brings a glory to God that is new and fresh. He delights in the thought of his children living in the truth. This is what it took to heal my divided heart. I had to know that the things I desired were not all counter to his will. He just had to be trusted enough by me to allow Him through the power of the Holy Spirit to restore everything that I believed would never come back. What he wanted for me at times was what I wanted for myself and even greater than that. But I had to get to the truth of submitting my desires to His Lordship. When I did that, I found in him a resting place. There was not a shortage of grace that would be extended if I fell and there was not a sword waiting to chop my head off or pierce me in the chest if I made a mistake. This was the reality that being born again had to give me. I had to learn from all the people that did me wrong, I was the one that was holding me back. I was the one who had myself in bondage. I would not forgive me, and this is the reason that I could not receive forgiveness.

It was foreign to me to be loved despite my flaws. I thought flaws should only be tolerated not celebrated. This is why I always hid in my power. I shrunk back into situations where I clearly should have stood up and said something. I knew that I was enough with Christ, but I felt I had to convince myself that it was ok to be enough. In my extremeness, I thought being too much was better than being enough.

I learned forgiveness is the gift you give before the error could be made amends for. It is the posture that says no matter what is done or what I lose, I still give myself and others grace to overcome every sin that causes heartache and loss. I have learned that the grace of God in Jesus was slain before the foundation of the world. This means that before the offenses could come or anyone could be fully responsible for their actions, there was a sufficient supply of grace from the cross that came to liberate you. Bondage is a mindset; it is a mental chain. The mind can be a mental prison, but thanks be to God that the word is a key that will liberate you from you. The you that would threaten to keep your heart hurting and your mind in confusion. Jesus promised He is not the author of confusion. Let's make up our mind today to ask him for forgiveness as we forgive others from our heart for the things that may have transpired in our lives.

Chapter 12

The Remedy

It was the Christ who chose the cross to save all who could not pay for the sins that they committed against God. This showed me how to forgive. Moreover, it was the Lord Jesus who taught me that I could live. Live and live again. It is never too late to begin again. I gained so much revelation and insight into life by listening to the downloads of the Holy Spirit in my heart. One of my most precious treasures in darkness was when I got a new revelation of who Jesus was. He is divine. He is the son of God. He is the lamb who takes away the sins of the world! But something supernatural happened to me to understand his human nature. One day after contemplating on the goodness of God I got the impression that only Holy Spirit can give. While thinking of His Holy name I began to hear to make the J silent and replace it with a H. Confused I said in my inner thoughts Hes-us. I kept saying it until I could comprehend what was being said. Hes-us. Hes-us! He's

Us!!! I realized that the revelation was becoming clearer and clearer. God became a man in the form of JESUS. He is in us, and we are like him. The word of God says as HE is, so are we in this world. We serve a high priest that knows what we go through because he put on human flesh and lived the human experience. HE is in us and through us we are one. The bible also says to those who asked him to show them the father. He said when you have seen me you have seen the father, and we are one.

Adam and Eve were the first Adam. Jesus was the second Adam! Now we through the power of the spirit of God are the regenerated man we are the third Adam. We have been given the power to become the sons of God. We have the right to the tree of Life. The earth has been waiting for us to manifest his Power and act in divine completeness. We are the 3rd day people when we believe in Jesus. When we call on his name for salvation, fully trusting him is when the fullness of time comes forth, we will rise to everlasting life because of what JESUS did when he died and rose again. This is the revelation that set me free. Many churches and religious organizations want to focus on changing people. Causing people to behave instead of surrender to the Lordship of Christ. They have done an awful thing to make humans think they could live perfectly on their own by behaving instead of changing and being transformed by the power of Christ. We all need forgiveness. Stop sinning, they will say but the only way to get free from sin is to have a relationship with Jesus through the Holy Spirit. This is how we change. It is not our own power. It is not correct to make sin the focus and not Jesus. We need to wake up and realize Jesus dealt with sin over 2000 years ago on the cross and when He got up out of the grave. We are free the moment we accept that and quit trying to play like we got it all together. No one is spotless unless he makes them new and gives them the power to overcome temptation and provide the way of escape when the enemy comes to trap us. He is God, and he traded places with us so that we could receive his judgement of well done. Instead of severe punishment for breaking the commandments of God. This journey of erasing the past man that I was to establish His story in the earth. He is the only important figure. Not just my story. It was just an episode that led to the truth. I had to go through it to find the testimony that I could be delivered from my confusion frustration and be changed to be more like Jesus. Someone willing to give and forgive those who hurt me most. It is never about what we did because what He did trumps it all! We have the power in Jesus' name to see ourselves as redeemed from every curse every addiction, and every shame.

On this journey I learned to take my eyes off me and what I went through. That is how I forget the past. There is hope in the cross.

Do you have the same struggles I had? If so, you may have been born that way in your mind you may believe that. With those thoughts people may have rejected you for all your life. Just know that Jesus has his arms wide open, and he wants you to know when you accept him the only thing that needs to change is your name. You are not a victim! You are Victorious in Christ! That is that your new name and put His. The punishment for everything that you can think of that you deserve death for, Jesus has the final say. He took on sin at the cross that you can receive new life in His name. He gave us his name. We got married to the mercy of God through the spirit of Jesus and just like a bride receives access to the benefits of being a married woman to the man that she said yes to, we have the same privileges. We have our new name! We suffered with him was buried with him and through the symbolism of water baptism in Jesus' name we have been given the chance to rise to newness of life and live forever more. Although I hurt for many years not feeling worthy of receiving love and forgiveness. I had to allow Jesus to knock the religion out of me and He himself gave me the yes in my soul to be obedient to his commandments. When I fall, as all of us do from time to time, I can remember the scripture that says a righteous man fall seven times, but He gets back up. I had to acknowledge that I had judged and condemned myself for the things I felt. Many of these feelings came from the trauma I experienced.

It is time to finally put that old story and that old narrative to rest. It is time for us as children of God to recognize our old life is gone, we are new, and we have been given access to all the power of Heaven in Jesus name. That is why we are called the bride of Christ. Not because we are so holy than thou because He had mercy on us and showed us what many refuse to see. He showed us He is for us. God with us. Emmanuel which means God with us. We are not alone. We don't have to suffer in this life alone. He is our partner. He comes along side us through the Holy Spirit to guide us. It does not matter who will not love you because you have tendencies that do not match the stereotype of the gender you were assigned at birth, which is your birthright. None of those matters! Get your mind out of the tug of war. Decide today that if Jesus died for me and rose again. I am going to rise and live for Him. If you do that and sincerely mean it, you have been born again. Now retrain yourself to only answer to the name He gave you. You never again have to feel ashamed or dirty or disgusting. He has come to bring Joy to your world.

You will go through things. Don't think for one second that becoming a believer exempts you from trouble. It doesn't. It will bring more negative occurrences at times because the world through religion will reject you according to the bible. They don't like what religion has taught them that we represent. The truth is you will make it to the finish line because, our Story is HIS STORY! We are a family. He is our father. HE will replace the dead beats and those who were ignorant fathers who caused so much pain and questions in our identity. The father is the one who affirms and speaks life into the son to become what he is destined to become. He can do that. His words are filled with affirmations that you can speak over yourself. Be not dismayed

God will take care of everything concerning you. He will perfect us. We need to quit seeking man's version of deliverance. That is the kind that said he took the taste of sin out of my mouth so that I can flaunt my freedom. In this place we brag about things like saying, "I don't desire to do this or that anymore." "I am cured!" The problem with that is there is an air of pride still in that statement. He died not to take anything from you, He died to give you the power to give up anything that would stand in the way of a right relationship with him. He died and rose again so you can know who you are in Christ which gives you abundant life.

No more becoming crazy trying to understand why you may have this lust problem which is a result of abuse early exposure to explicit things. Believe that you can change. This issue will either go away or you will receive power to no longer repeat the negative cycles that you have found yourself in.

Chapter 13

The Power of Your Birth Right

The enemy of your soul wants men to give up the right to be men. There is power in the role of being a man. The authority of God gives men the right to lead. This is a great gift. Sometimes when you lead there are challenges, but it should only show you what Jesus put inside of you to overcome each challenge you may face. You are strong enough to endure anything. The bible says in Philippians 4:13, "I can do all things through Christ who gives me strength." You have His strength if you struggle with feeling strong. He will give you everything you need to live a Godly life. He will even give you the power to stand up and tell the devil No, I will never serve you and give my mind to your games and tricks.

Truth be told he made men and he made women. As men we must learn in the process of maturity, we are different than women. We have a biological need for sexual contact. It has been medically proven that men need sex. Coming from the church background I thought it was wrong to desire sexual contact which was an appetite that was awaken early. But that is not totally truth. We naturally are wired to think sexual thoughts and long for a wife to fulfill those desires with. I thought for every desire I will be going to hell. I was going crazy trying to deal with lustful desires on my own. We must become vulnerable and share our lessons with others, so they won't fall victim to the same lies the enemy told us. The truth is it is about commitment and the covenant of marriage being a safe place to explore the holy desire for sex in man. God made us to be sexual only in the commitment of marriage. As a truth, we must understand God's design all men contain in his loins a factory of seeds. We have the power to make millions of sperm cells. These seeds are driven more by the testosterone that God gives us that we release through sexual connection with our wives. Having a factory of seeds, and the natural need to release, it makes sense that if a man did not enjoy making love there would never be any children created. God in his infinite wisdom gave us a drive to make us fulfill our God given mandate to make more children and replenish the earth. Then He gave us marriage to protect us from the drive becoming out of control which leads to disasters and sexually transmitted diseases and children that we don't raise which causes us to be hated and despised. It is our divine obligation to manage that responsibility to replenish the earth within a healthy and safe sacred space.

Now that we understand in our body that we have an animalistic instinct to see and like what we like. We can get rid of the men are dog narratives. We may have animalistic instincts, but we have a mind to know how to not do things that are out of bounds. I have never seen a dog who saw his food and water and thought all day about eating it and restraining himself when he is hungry. No, that doesn't occur. He is naturally attracted to what he needs to survive. He goes and gets the food without thinking about the dangers or traps someone may have set for him. The same would have been the truth for men. Except God gave us logic and reasoning to not destroy ourselves with our desires. However, we are naturally attracted to sex because of its power is to produce. This fire can be heightened by childhood abuse. This is also a sign that we need healing.

Now we can argue all day about this or that or how God made us and what we shouldn't do, I believe it is not our job to recreate ourselves it is the will of God that gives us these abilities. On the other hand, it is our job that we must manage the drives and appetites that we naturally have so that they don't bring us shame and pain. We must heal our minds because religion and other dogmatic people groups will convince us that our sexual desires are all so evil. Jesus came to make us free from wrong thinking. He has the power to give us HOLY Sexuality. The kind of sexual experiences that lead to life and not death. Hebrews 13 tells us that, "Marriage is Honorable in all, and the marriage bed is undefiled." NO sin takes place between two married people who comes together and have sex. It is all free game. God is glorified when the husband and wife enjoys connecting physically and sexually. The bible shows that there is nothing bad in and of itself if we do things God's way, we are free and clear to operate. We must have a marriage license which gives us the authority to partake in sexual activities in the legal and righteous way which is in marriage. We must recognize that we are three-part beings. The only thing is, is that the flesh or human side of us will get us into trouble if we think irrationally and not put boundaries around our appetites. I can't eat 4 pizzas every day for lunch and dinner and walk away with the belief that I deserve to stay fit and not fat, especially if I never work out. The truth is as healthy as your hunger is to sustain life in you, every appetite was given by God to enjoy. Abuse may have tainted the waters that God wanted you to freely drink of, but He will restore you if you trust Him to teach and instruct you in his ways. There must be moderation and balance and not overindulgence. You don't have to get religious and turn into a prudish person. You can love Jesus and we as men must have wisdom.

Now men and I am speaking exclusively to men, we know when we need release. God has provided an answer for that problem. Marriage is a solution. We still must understand that we are working with our wives. This means we must be considerate of her feelings, thoughts and emotions and her physical condition. We can't override her to get what we want. We must honor God. The Holy Spirit will give us wisdom. God is a merciful God slow to anger. I pray I will be used by Jesus and wisdom in the hopes of freeing my brothers from self-imposed bondage. How else would you manage your seed if you don't have another outlet in your wife. People will preach to you and condemn you and not explain and teach you how to operate in your divine gifting.

This is our blessing that we must do it God's way to have his blessing. We can't legally ethically, and spiritually have sex with others outside of marriage covenant and think God is pleased.

That would be considered as a license to sin which no one needs. We need a marriage license. I got my healing when I stopped being foolish and believing that I could live without a sexual release. I tried to rewrite the plan of God because of shame and self-condemnation. Being a believer we are not under condemnation. There is no condemnation for us who are in Christ Jesus who do according to what His word tells us to do. I don't care how saved you are when your back itches you make away to get it scratched. But do it God's way, your answer is in marriage. Christ centered marriage. Husbands, you need a wife! You may not understand now but as the Holy Spirit reveals this is His protection you will understand. This is wisdom on the human side of life. I found that we as people like to sneak around and do forbidden things. Some of us feel like being married is boring. You need an imagination to fully enjoy God's gift. Take that desire for multiple people and create the fantasy of your choice with your spouse. That is how to get the spark back after feeling bored.

God knows what he made when he made a man. Now as for the ladies I don't claim to know anything about women. But I have heard that women need emotional connection. I also heard that many women have different needs. We as men must be sensitive to your needs learning you is our lifelong mission. So, brothers quit trying to be like women. We are two different and distinct creations.

Deal with life by managing it and teach your sons how to be responsible with their seed. Retrain yourself to be responsible with that seed because one of those will eventually become heir to your inheritance.

Responsible people know that you must have an outlet to have fun occasionally. I am glad that God has provided me a wife. This type of activity is approved of in the confines of a covenant of marriage between a man a woman. Everything else is spiritually out of bounds and sure to cause you headache that you would never have to endure should you choose to obey and do it God's way. Pace yourself don't move to fast and miss the blessing of God my brothers. There is a prize at the finish line. God will help us reclaim our authentic identity and become whole sexually even after abuse if that is your story.

Lord, help us, we are all in flesh. There is pressure on all of us. Let us protect our queens making sure that all the pressure does not go on your wife. Turn her on and she has the power to turn you out in pleasure. Be sensitive to her needs and you will see the blessing of the Lord that makes us rich and adds no sorrow! Be patient, especially, if she has other issues that she deals with, and at times she may not be able to meet your needs but pray together and God will provide an answer for both of your needs. Even in events like medical issues or other pressing matters. Even in marriage we must discipline yourself so that you can endure in a godly manner, you should be able to be an understanding husband. Make sure you respect your wife and do not violate her body against her will. Sometimes being in a Godly marriage requires that you understand on another level more than some will have to. Especially if there are issues that she is battling with, and she does not feel like stroking your ego because she feels depleted.

Lastly, I hope my transparency and choosing to be

real and exposing the inside my and other men's issues was handled skillfully and is going to result in growth and understanding of complex issues after overcoming cycles of pain and abuse. I just know a house divided will not stand. We must work together in healing. Now we can get up and thank God that he gave us relief and safety to do with your spouse what must be done. We can enjoy and still be saved in the morning because we obeyed the order of God. We can be sexual, and we still love God. Erase that shame and become a new creature in Christ Jesus! Enjoy each other with every inch of each other's body. Get creative and find a life of fulfillment within your marriage bed. God is being worshiped when we follow the rules, and he will bless us for our obedience. Amen

Chapter 14

A Higher Wisdom

One thing that causes us a Christians who are carriers of the truth to argue back and forth on issues and not agreeing with each other is there are levels of truth. For a baby, the best thing since so to speak is sliced bread is milk. It is not until you mature that your desire food that is bigger, stronger and takes teeth to break down, which are meat and vegetables. We argue on different subjects because some of us has a level of understanding that is pure and not hard to understand by complex thinkers which I would say is like milk, while the others may have a level of meat. Meat is being used in this example as a type of food that takes maturity to digest. Which means the person who only can digest milk are those who are fed and nourished on the level of a baby. Babies are not mature enough to eat strong solid foods. They are still able to survive on just milk. They grow on milk but the mature desire meat. The bible says earnestly desire the sincere milk of the word that you may grow thereby. The milk seems like enough to satisfy a mature person, until they can digest meat. As a babe in Christ, you must understand that what you believe in this stage may be incorrect in another level of your Christian journey. This is a wisdom that we must all understand to get along and not accuse each other of false teaching. Just because one part of the body believes in something that you do not believe in, we still are a viable part of the body of Christ if we have been born again.

For example, some of us believe we must pray before we leave the house every day and anoint ourselves with oil so we will be covered by the blood of Jesus and be safe from the attack of the enemy. The other of us believe that God supernaturally covers us instantly the moment we become believers without daily prayer before exiting our home and to this group they may believe it doesn't take all that prayer and anointing oil. The bottom line is in matters that are not life or death, we have a grace and capacity to believe and understand on different levels. This should cause us to come together and forebear one another in love. Just because my faith may be different than yours, if my heart is to please Jesus and keep the faith I should, in the spirit of Love, provide understanding that we as brothers and sisters in Christ can both co-exist. We don't have to throw the baby out when we throw the bath water out. We can believe and still disagree. For years I believed that the goal of a

Christian was to make disciples and win souls to Christ. Now that I am at another level of thinking because of teaching of the word of God I now know that no one can come to Jesus to be born again if the spirit of God doesn't draw them to himself. It is not mere human effort. I thought it was my mission to preach! Preach! Preach to everyone in my own strength! I found out my living for God and being an example of daily discipleship in Christ will out do my preaching. This is why we can't say that a person who is not always witnessing is not a true believer. We all have been given a measure of faith for our lives. Some people believe you should get saved and get married and stop making excuses about trying to find the right one. The one who believes that is one who may have found the scripture that marriage is honorable in all, and the bed is undefiled. The other person may believe you must wait until the appropriate time. The truth both are right but in different seasons and different times. They both could be right and wrong at the same time. God knows our faith level that he gave us. We must keep the faith for what He is doing in our lives and not make others agree with us more than we have capacity to see.

God is the judge we need to stop judging each other negatively and focus our attention on bearing fruit unto the Lord and not tearing down each other's character for what we don't believe or do believe. We are never to debate with each other because the Spirit of God has given us the mindset to agree even when we disagree. That is maturity. When we learn how to work together and love each other and accept differing opinions. The way we grow is together not apart. I thank God for the leadership lessons I learned, while feeling hurt by the church. My misunderstanding is what created most of the confusion. The pastors and leaders and even my parents never even knew I was upset with some of the things I thought that leaders were intentionally causing pain, but they were not. The enemy of my soul wanted to deceive me and keep me from the leader so that the anointing would not flow from the head. Freedom is knowing that God is in charge, and He will right the wrong if we allow Him to correct our ways of thinking. Our ways are not His ways we must believe that God is doing the work, and we are just vehicles to get things done. I said all that to say this. There is a spirit behind the scenes at work. We must fight to stand against the spirit of this wicked age that causes us to fall away and stay disconnected from the very people that God wants to use to bring us deliverance. We have power, but the power we possess is wasted if we intend to use it to disarm one another.

I have learned that there are hidden agents of Darkness behind the LGBTQIA identity or the alphabet people as I call them. This spirit exposes himself by utilizing biblical symbols to confuse many into thinking that the feelings that the individual find themselves struggling with is alright to indulge in it. For example, there is the queer sign of a rainbow which originally was God's promise to never destroy the world by water. Also, the parade that most of the queer community attend to find a sense of belonging and celebration is called Pride! Which is how Satan fell from heaven… Pride. Pride goes before a fall and the spirit behind the lust behind the identity of queerness may not be everyone who lives that lifestyle truth some people genuinely are identifying with this lifestyle because of the feeling they believe that they always had. This is not all truth but their truth. The issue with this is if I believe in my mind that if I jump from the 3rd story of a building without help or safety measures that I won't be injured can be my truth if my mind is not thinking rationally, But the truth is that my truth is not the absolute truth. My reality will find out when I make the wrong choice to test gravity and jump. Too many people have taken that leap and become stuck with the consequences of jumping into that lifestyle and sickness or despair has ensued. It is not any one's fault for how they feel but we must manage wrong feelings and emotions if we want to live long healthy lives. But we as believer know that everything that is in opposition against God is motivated by the spirit of the enemy. He is attempting to destroy the person with their own desires.

He is tricky and a master deceiver. The deliverance comes when we finally know the truth and submit to God's word. God is not a man that he should lie. He made man with the ability to multiply when man and woman comes together. Anything else is against not only God but nature. We must know that anything that opposes the creation and design of God will bring unnecessary judgement and punishment. It is not God who has to punish those of us who are deceived in our minds to think this way it is life that is showing us The Truth. He is showing us because we are not following the things that life is teaching us which is how to avoid temptation and live instead of falling into death and despair.

Now the reality is, there are people who naturally are bent toward same sex attraction and gender identity disorders in their understanding. This can be true to them, but I believe the environmental factors whatever they were played a part. Whether through abuse or verbally spoken negative words from childhood, or from environmental factors or from direct spiritual attack from the womb before we are born, all of these are just a few ways that this spirit of error finds a resting place in the minds of people.

I have learned that spirits are so cunning they live to make us believe that the lies that are in our minds are a result of us thinking these thoughts. But it is not us! Many things can contribute to the way we think. We don't think like that! Most times if not all the times we think in a way that dishonors God and put us into harmful ways that thinking is a result of an evil spirit in us that is warring against obeying God. That is trying to kill us from the desires that we have. Our body is being used by demonic thoughts through our minds. The feelings of attractions are natural, but the unnatural desire to do things that are not appropriate comes from forces that are not of this world. It is that old ugly devil that wants us to destroy our own lives by indulging in things that are not for us. Once you get set free and delivered by Christ to see the truth, you will see and know the difference. Keep seeking my friend! I pray that this book will be the first step in your erasing the past, and that you allow God to use his fingers to rewrite your story, this will be an epic display of God's handiwork it is His/Story that is for His glory. Which means that the old you will be gone and behold he will make all things new including you.

-The End-

~My prayer for everyone reading this book~

Father, I pray for the one who is reading this book. I pray that they have learned many lessons that you have given me in my life story and experiences. I thank you for the power to teach the truth. I thank you that the word of God in this book will prick the hearts of many and make them ready to cry out to you and receive eternal life! I pray you give them the heart's desire and strength to overcome every lustful and strong desire that came through the wounds of trauma. I pray that your will for them to be made new will come to past. These are your children, and they have desired to be free. Give them a testimony! Let them rewrite their name as victorious not victim because you have declared that everyone who Jesus saves will have a new name, because they have a new destiny. May your holy spirit indwell them and may they always be blessed to overcome the strategies, plots, and plans of the enemy. Give them power to overcome that nothing by any means shall harm them. Give them the ability to walk over the traps set to take them out. Most importantly let them know that you are with them and that they have already overcome in your name, because you are in them the greater one who has already overcome this world for them. Greater is He that is in them than he that is in the world opposing the truth of God in their minds. Help them to cast down every argument that tries to exalt itself against the knowledge of God! Thank you, Father, for all the blessings granted in Salvation in Jesus' mighty name we pray, Amen.

Made in the USA
Columbia, SC
17 June 2024

d914a854-aec5-493f-b50a-2790044154a9R02